VICTORIA AND ALBERT MUSEUM

Published by V & A Publications
First published in 1986
© Trustees of the Victoria and Albert Museum
ISBN 1 85177 132 8

10 9 8 7 6

Written by Anthony Burton
Printed in Great Britain

FRONT COVER: (left to right) *English tricycle horse, about 1915;
German teddy bear, about 1935; eighteenth-century English dolls'
house; German tin train, about 1860; early twentieth-century Indian
puppet from Rajasthan; miniature Staffordshire cup and saucer, early
nineteenth century; board for 'Game of the Goose', home-made in
England about 1800; Indian tiger of painted wood, early twentieth
century; eighteenth-century Dutch and English silver toys; clown
from a circus made by Schoenhut, U.S.A., about 1920; nineteenth-
century spinning top; German pressed tin Ferris wheel, about 1910;
miniature Staffordshire cup and saucer, about 1830; English doll and
chair, about 1680.*

BACK COVER: *Children's outfits of the 1930s (boy's linen smock,
girl's velvet dress); English child's pedal car, about 1920.*

PREVIOUS PAGE: *As visitors enter the main hall of the Museum,
they are greeted by a 'frontispiece' with pictures of children at play
through the ages.*

Contents

5   Introduction

7   Traditional Toys

10   Horses

12   Trains, Cars, Clockwork

14   Optical Toys

16   Toy Soldiers

17   Soft Toys

18   Puppets and Toy Theatre

20   Games

25   Dolls' Houses

28   Dolls

34   The Social History of Childhood

42   The History of the Museum

46   The Museum at Work

(Right) *Creative art work in the Saturday workshops for children.*

(Below) *School parties visiting the museum can participate (by advance booking) in a programme of study sessions. Here children have an opportunity to handle some old toys.*

Introduction

What happens to us as children influences us for the rest of our lives. So we all have good reason to preserve memories of our own childhood. The Bethnal Green Museum tries to preserve something of everybody's childhood, and it is a museum that should appeal to everybody – for there is no-one who was not once a child.

Our happiest memory of childhood, probably, is of playing. The wonderful experiences of 'messing about' and 'fooling around' cannot be put in a museum; but playthings can. So the brightest and most attractive feature of the museum is the collection of playthings – toys, dolls, dolls' houses, games, puppets – ranging from the seventeenth century to the present. This collection is displayed in the three lower galleries of the museum. As you come in, toys are on the right, dolls' houses straight ahead, and dolls and games on the left.

All these exhibits are locked up in glass cases: for we are a traditional museum. Still, we have arranged the galleries as playfully as we can. There is no compulsory way to go round this museum. You are encouraged to wander. The showcases are not in straight lines, but placed so as always to beckon you round another corner. (And yet you cannot get lost in the big, open building.) Even if the visitors cannot play with the exhibits, they can let their eyes play over the brightly coloured displays.

The exhibits are in fact arranged in logical groups, and each showcase has a 'star-board', a notice telling you what we hope you will most want to know about the exhibits. Every exhibit also has a small caption with more detail for the specialist.

Another cherished memory of childhood is of stories. The museum has a huge library of historic children's books. The visitor does not see this, except in the form of special exhibitions, which are regularly drawn from it. Up-to-date children's books are now easily available in public libraries, and the museum does not try to compete with these. Its library of historic children's books (the

Renier Collection) is kept for the use of scholars and researchers.

On the top floor of the museum are two more galleries, and here, gradually, a third section of the museum is taking shape. This is devoted to the social history of childhood. The core of it is the collection of children's dress, from the eighteenth century to the present. Around this all kinds of things and pictures connected with childhood are being gathered.

How the museum came to be here is described on p. 42. Ever since it began to specialize in childhood in the 1920s, it has arranged activities and events for children. Especially, it tries to provide opportunities for children to express in creative art the pleasure they have felt in looking at the exhibits. The activities change all the time, so we will not describe them further here.

What remains largely the same (though displays change sometimes) is the collection of exhibits, so the rest of this book is about them. Do they always remain silent and motionless behind glass? Or, when the front door has closed in the evening behind the last visitor, do the showcases fly open, and toys scramble out to play? Visitors, unfortunately, will never know.

Traditional Toys

At the start of the gallery to the right of the entrance.

No-one can doubt that from the earliest times people have made playthings from whatever came to hand: mud and straw, sticks and stones, rags and bones. These were what they used to make all sorts of things which they needed in order to survive. And when they relaxed from this hard work, they doubtless used the same materials to make miniature models of the people, animals and things around them. This is the greatest attraction of toys: they show us the world in miniature.

Archaeologists have dug up miniature objects from many ancient civilizations. It is not certain that these were playthings. They may have been magical objects (especially if they were found in tombs), intended to give their owners the power to control the full-size world. All toys have this magic to some extent: they help children to realize their own powers, and to adjust to the grown-up world.

The Bethnal Green Museum is not a museum of archaeology and so it does not have toys from ancient civilizations. The earliest toys in its collections are from the seventeenth century, the time when toy-making began to be a craft by which people could earn a living. Once, every father would make toys for his own children, but by the end of the seventeenth century a small toy industry was established in several regions of Germany, with Nuremberg as a trading centre.

Craftsmen were organized in guilds, according to their trades, and many of them copied their usual products on a small scale, as toys. The museum's Nuremberg dolls' house of 1673 (one of the first things to be seen in the toy gallery) contains the entire paraphernalia of ordinary life in miniature. Because it was easiest to make toys from wood, it was wood carvers and wood turners (craftsmen who used a lathe) who specialised in cheap toys. Naturally it was in forest

A typical nineteenth-century German Noah's Ark.

regions, where wood was available, that they worked. Toy-making went on in the Alps, in the Grödner Tal on the Italian side and at Oberammergau and Berchtesgaden on the northern side; in the Meiningen uplands around Sonneberg in Thuringia; and in Saxony, in the Erzgebirge region. Toys from these areas were exported all over Europe, via Nuremberg and Leipzig.

The toymakers of Germany made wooden dolls, of course, together with jumping jacks, roundabouts, horses and carriages, horseback sol-

diers, foot-soldiers on crisscross expandable frames, birds, animals, and little buildings. The charm of these lies not only in their crisp carving, but in their swiftly painted decoration; and the painters were as important as the woodworkers in the German trade. These bright little toys make their strongest impression when they are put together to form a large composite toy, such as a Noah's Ark or a Christmas pyramid. In the pyramid, Nativity figures are supported on a two- or three-tiered structure, which revolves when hot

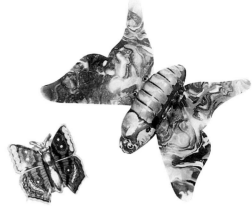

air rises from lighted candles and moves vanes at the top. Large and small, these toys were produced by home-workers in ever larger quantities for very poor wages, until the depression and wars of the twentieth century weakened the trade.

Many of the toys exported from Germany were of timelessly traditional types, and similar toys are to be found in the museum's displays of Indian, Russian and Mexican folk toys. Folk toys and cheap toys perish all too easily, while big expensive toys survive more successfully to find a place in museums. This museum is better off for foreign folk toys (which must have seemed unusual to those who collected them and gave them to the museum) than for the kind of toy that would once have been commonplace among the children of this country. The Museum does not possess, for instance, 'Bartholomew babies' (toys of the kind sold at Bartholomew Fair and other fairs), or the little cottonwool sheep now known

only in the nursery rhyme 'Young lambs to sell', or toys made of gutta percha (a nineteenth-century forerunner of rubber), or paper windmills. The 'penny toys' which best survive are those made of painted tin, which are relatively sturdy.

(Above far left) *A carriage and horses, probably made at Berchtesgaden around 1800. This toy has a box made of thin slices of wood, steamed and bent into a characteristic round-cornered shape. Inside the box lid, all the toy's owners, from 1803 onwards, have written their names. Such boxes, plain or painted, were used for all kinds of German toys.*

(Below left) *A tiny rocking horse, a traditional toy from Thuringia.*

(Below centre) *A pull-along bird, mounted on a bellows which, when pushed down, blows air through a whistle to produce the bird's cry.*

(Above right) *Cheap tin toys made in Germany, 1900-1920.*

(Below right) *Whittled and painted ladies, popular toys in nineteenth-century Russia, made chiefly at Bogorodskoye.*

(Above) *Alfred Fuller, aged four in 1836, with the hobby-horse which previously belonged to his father Richard.*

(Below) *An English rocking-horse, of about 1910, covered in hide and slung on a frame.*

Horses

Around the imitation roundabout in the toy gallery

Until the invention of the motor car, a boy's favourite toy would probably have been a horse. The hobby horse (a horse's head on a stick which a child straddled) was popular in the Middle Ages, as we know from illustrations, though none survives from so early. The museum has one dating from the eighteenth century: its tiny head is carved on the knotty end of the stick. We have a portrait of the little boy in blue to whom it belonged in 1836.

Realistic horses carved in wood and often covered in hide were known by the end of the sixteenth century. If they were on wheels they could be pushed or pulled along by a child learning to walk. Smaller horses drawing carts or coaches, or equipped with stables to live in, would appeal to older children, as examples of the world in miniature. Horses were generally too big to be conveniently transported long distances, so even while the German toy trade dominated Europe, it did not deal much in horses, which were made locally.

Rocking horses first appeared in the seventeenth century. The simplest, unrealistic kind is made of two roughly semicircular sides joined by a seat, with a head and tail added. This type, refined and decorated, remained usual in Germany through the nineteenth century. In England, however, the sleek racer, with outstretched legs attached at the hooves to long, curling rockers was the favourite. The type of rocking horse that is slung from a frame was devised in 1880. Dual-purpose horses were mounted on wheeled bases which could be bolted on to rockers. In the later nineteenth-century horses were combined with tricycles to make velocipedes. Often stylishly carved and painted grey with conventional dappling, horses are not easy to date, but most were made in the late nineteenth and early twentieth centuries. The museum collection contains most varieties.

(Above) *A toy stage-coach and horses, made in England probably in the 1830s.*

(Below) *A toy horse and coal-cart, made in England in 1913.*

Trains, Cars, Clockwork

Half-way along the toy gallery, near the stairs

Transport toys closely imitate real forms of transport. So when steam passenger trains began in Germany in 1835, toymakers carved little wooden trains. But trains seemed much more realistic if made of metal, and this became possible owing to a new technique of mass production: toys were made by stamping out their parts from sheets of tin plate by power presses. Nuremberg, where toy-making and metalworking both had long traditions, naturally became the centre of this manufacture. At first tin toys had to be painted by hand, but later detailed colourful designs were printed on the tin by lithography.

Trains, motor-cars and boats were produced in great quantity by German firms such as Bing, Märklin, Lehmann and Carette. Tin toys were made also in France, America and England (where Hornby and Bassett Lowke were the best known names).

Transport toys were often powered by clockwork motors. These could be applied to many other kinds of mechanical toy, including figures of men or animals. Fernand Martin of Paris made many little men in the late nineteenth century, the 'gay violinist' being one of the most popular. In the 1930s Marx of New York and Shuco of Nuremberg made similar toys.

A slightly different way of making metal toys was by die-casting. This was the technique pioneered by Hornby in Dinky toys, and used also for Lesney's 'Matchbox' vehicles.

Unlike wooden horses, almost all these metal toys can be precisely identified and dated, for they have makers' marks, and the manufacturers issued catalogues of their products. So they have become collectors' pieces. The museum has quite a variety of examples, but does not try to rival the dedicated collectors.

A train layout by Hornby in the Toy Gallery.

(Top) *An engine and tender made by Carette of Nuremberg, about 1910.*

(Centre left to right) *Clockwork toys. 'Le gai violoniste' by Martin of Paris, about 1900; 'Schuco' clowns by Schreyer of Nuremberg, about 1935; 'Gertie the galloping goose' by the Unique Art Manufacturing Co. of Newark, U.S.A., about 1930.*

(Bottom left) *A clockwork car made by Bing in Germany in the 1920s.*

(Bottom right) *An early die-cast model: 'Bluebird' (after the car in which Malcolm Campbell broke the land speed record), made by William Britain and Co. in 1935-40. Until Dinky Toys came to dominate the market in the 1930s, die-cast vehicles were made as a side-line by firms, such as Britain's, specializing in lead soldiers.*

Optical Toys

At the far end of the toy gallery

Optical toys are toys which play tricks with the eye. Perhaps the best known – and a favourite still, ever since its invention in about 1817 – is the Kaleidoscope.

The simplest and earliest optical toys were adaptations of engraved pictures. The aim was to make them look more realistic. Peepshows gave greater depth to pictures by, as it were, separating them into slices and spacing out the slices. The Museum has important early peepshows produced by the Augsburg print publisher Martin Engelbrecht. The later ones (showing, for example, the Great Exhibition of 1851) work in exactly the same way. Another way of adding interest to a print was by shining light on it from the front and then the back, so that it changed appearance, either because it was really a sandwich of two slightly differing prints, or because it had pin-pricks which let the light through to give an effect like lamps at night. One device for viewing such prints was called a Polyorama Panoptique.

Automata

Toys that move by themselves are usually worked by some kind of clockwork mechanism. Clockwork has been used in watches and small clocks since the fifteenth century. It was only in the later nineteenth century that mass-produced clockwork motors made cheap toys possible. Before that, mechanical toys were produced, but they were expensive, and for adults. They are usually called 'Automata'. The Museum has examples made in Germany and France. This monkey, made in Germany, about 1875, plucks his mandoline, turns his head, opens his mouth and moves his eyes.

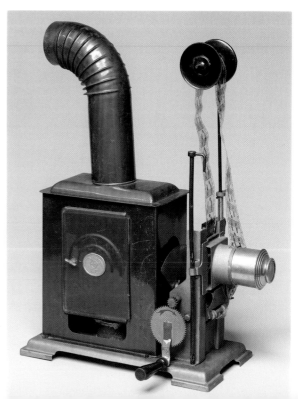

(Top far right) *The Phenikistiscope, or Phantascope. The viewer spins the disc and peeps through its slots at the reflections in the mirror. The figures seem to move as he watches.*

(Right) *A cinematograph of about 1902 by the German maker Ernst Planck. It is a magic lantern with an attachment so that either glass slides or film can be shown.*

(Far right) *Transfer-printed slides for a toy magic lantern, made in Germany in the 1890s.*

Most later optical toys made use of a phenomenon called 'persistence of vision', first described in 1824. The Thaumotrope (1826) first exploited this in a very simple way (easier done than described). Then came devices – the Fantascope (1832), the Zoetrope (1834) and the Praxinoscope (1877) – which made a series of pictures spin round quickly but confined the viewer's vision to a single point so that the succession of images gave the impression of movement. The same principle is used in modern movie films.

But in films, the principle is combined with the Magic Lantern, a means of projecting transparent pictures at a distance by a powerful light. This was known from the seventeenth century, but improved in the nineteenth century, when lantern slides were invented which produced pictures that could move in simple but ingenious ways.

The Museum has examples of all these contrivances, together with many later toys which try to imitate, at a childish level, the cinematograph projector or the television. Optical toys were very popular in the Victorian period because they were not only amusing, but improving and educational for they taught a child some elementary science.

Toy Soldiers

*In the fort beyond the doll gallery to the left of
the entrance*

Little toy soldiers (made of lead, later of tin or an
alloy of tin and antimony, and nowadays of less
poisonous substances) have had a long history:
some scattered examples survive from the Middle
Ages. It was in the later eighteenth century that
they became very popular, the Hilpert family of
Nuremberg being the pioneer manufacturers,
from the 1760s on. Later, around 1840, came
Heinrichsen of Nuremberg and Allgeyer of
Fürth, who in 1848 settled on a standard size for
tin figures, the 'Nuremberg scale': 3cm for stand-
ing people, 4cm for horsemen. Their figures were
produced from moulds but were almost two-
dimensional, with details in shallow relief, and
are consequently known as 'flats'. Fully rounded
figures were occasionally produced, but were too
heavy and expensive to be popular. In 1893 William Britain of England invented a method of
casting hollow rounded figures, and Britains
have dominated the toy soldier trade ever since.

Toy soldiers quickly became collectors' items
because they are of standard dimensions but
have great variety of detail. There are well organized collectors' associations all over the world.
Not everyone is interested in minute differences
in military uniform, but manufacturers have always produced, alongside soldiers, figures representing all kinds of animals and people. These
can be a charming record of real life, the most
delightful being the German ones of the first half
of the nineteenth century.

(From top to bottom)

*Tournament knights with movable arms: flats by Heinrichsen of
Nuremberg, 1850-70.*

Early twentieth-century die-cast soldiers, mostly by Britains.

*Playing with soldiers is more fun if you have a fort. This one, of wood
and printed paper, is probably German, of about 1910.*

*Coster's cart and figures: die-cast models by Taylor & Barrett,
London, in the 1930s.*

Soft Toys

Near the horses

Soft toys must surely always have been made by mothers skilful at sewing, and must always have worn out very quickly. The recorded history of soft toys more or less begins with the products of the Steiff firm, begun by Margarete Steiff in 1880, and still the leading producers of these toys. All kinds of cuddly animals have been made as soft toys. The Teddy Bear first appeared in 1903, the golliwog in the 1890s. Mass-produced soft toys have often been based on characters in newspaper cartoons, films or children's books: Snoopy, Paddington Bear and Mickey Mouse are still well known, while Pepi, Bonzo, and Pip, Squeak and Wilfred were favourites with an older generation. Outstanding in the museum's collection is a set of soft toys made by the Cattley family, with an extensive wardrobe, and a series of photographs and watercolours recording their life.

(Above) *Some of the Cattley toys in a watercolour painted by Constance Emily Cattley in 1908.*

(Below) *A group of the museum's teddies.*

Puppets and Toy Theatre

Along the back wall of the museum

Mass-produced toys can usually be briefly described in general terms, but this is not true of puppets. Most of the best puppets were individually made by showmen for special plays, so tend to be different from each other.

There are four types of puppets: glove puppets, string puppets (or marionettes), rod puppets and shadow puppets. Puppets are popular throughout the world, and their origin is lost in the distant past. Some countries have long traditions and a limited repertoire of plays. The one-stringed marionettes of India, the subtly jointed string-puppets of Burma, the *bunraku* puppets of Japan (each operated by three men), and the brightly costumed glove puppets of China all obey firm rules in performance. The nearest equivalent to these traditional forms in Europe is, perhaps, the Punch and Judy show. This derives from the Italian commedia dell'arte, and the most precious exhibit in the museum's puppet gallery is an eighteenth-century Italian theatre, with exquisite puppets representing Harlequin, Pantaloon and some other characters of the commedia dell'arte. Modern puppeteers throughout Europe have developed in highly individual ways. Polish, Czech and German puppets are shown (including shadow puppets by Lotte Reiniger) as well as English puppets by Gair Wilkinson, W. H. Whanslaw, Mary Bligh Bond and John Bickerdike.

Toy theatres, printed on paper, stuck to card, and cut out, were popular throughout Europe in the nineteenth century, though the English publishers produced the most versatile kits, with play scripts and all the characters and scenery to match. These theatres often copied productions in the real theatre quite closely, so they are both toys and historical documents. The museum displays fully constructed toy theatres and also many of the printed sheets in their uncut form.

Many exhibits among the puppets and toy theatres have been lent by the Theatre Museum.

(Above) *A bunraku puppet, made in Japan probably at the end of the nineteenth century.*

(Left) *Japanese, Indian and Chinese puppets on display in the Puppet Gallery.*

(Right) *The Punch and Judy show of Gus Wood, who worked as a showman from 1912 until 1962.*

(Below) *A Turkish puppet made of hide.*

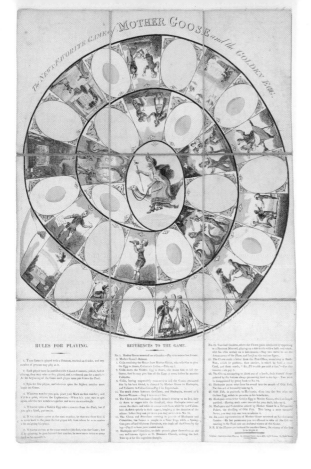

Games

Beyond the fort

Board games like chess, draughts, backgammon and solitaire (which have roots far back in history) are, perhaps, rather for adults than children, so the museum only has a few examples.

Simpler table games with pictorial boards are, however, a good way of amusing children quietly. The most popular kind of game requires the players to move counters along a marked course, their progress being governed by the scores they achieve when throwing a dice or twirling a teetotum. These 'race' games are all variants on 'The Game of the Goose', as the oldest form was called (for no very good reason). The race could have obstacles or short cuts built into it, like snakes and ladders. It could also be adapted to convey instruction painlessly; and so many nineteenth-century race games follow a path through geography, history or morals. When, in the twentieth century, race games become less earnest, they can still offer interesting sidelights on contemporary developments, such as cycling. Games of this kind depend quite heavily on words, so are not easily exportable. The museum's collection is therefore almost entirely of English games, and is rich in early engraved, hand-coloured games produced by such firms as Wallis, Harris and Darton (who also published children's books). Later well-known publishers were Jaques, Raphael Tuck and Chad Valley.

Playing cards for children have also often been given an educational slant, though most are based on the 'snap' or 'Happy Family' principles. Purely pictorial cards which could be combined in an infinite number of ways to make panoramas, faces or figures, were more exportable, so the museum has a more international collection. Similarly with jigsaws, which were invented in eighteenth-century England as 'dissected puzzles'.

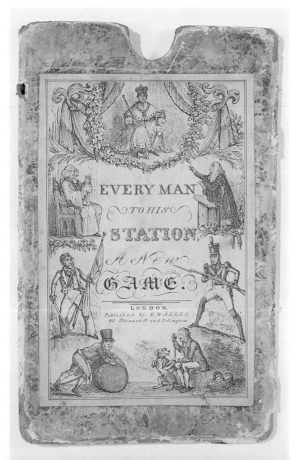

(Top) *The Game of the Goose originated in sixteenth-century Italy. This version, a hand-coloured etching, was published by John Wallis of London in 1808.*

(Bottom) *The slipcase for a board game published around the 1820s by E. Wallis. Game sheets of this period were mounted on linen in sections so that they could be folded away in a case.*

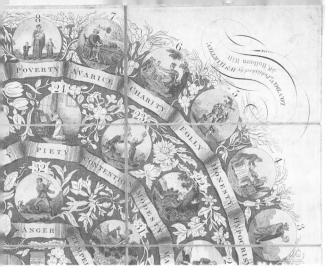

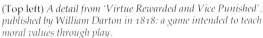

(Top left) *A detail from 'Virtue Rewarded and Vice Punished', published by William Darton in 1818: a game intended to teach moral values through play.*

(Top right) *Examples from a set of forty four 'Happy Families' cards made by John Jaques about 1860: hand-coloured woodcuts after designs by Sir John Tenniel.*

(Right) *'Laripino', about 1935, is one of the wide range of table games made by J. W. Spear & Sons of Enfield.*

(Bottom left) *The game of 'The Produce and Manufactures of … England and Wales' was designed to teach geography. It was published about 1850 by J. Passmore, Wallis's successor.*

(Bottom Right) *Chad Valley's 'Our Boys' compendium series contained some of the firm's most popular games. This example dates from about 1912.*

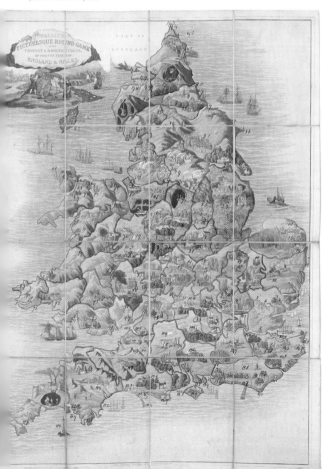

(Above) *Butcher's shops seem to be a specially English toy. Quite a few survive from the nineteenth century, all very much alike. Usually they are in glass-fronted boxes (like this one), and are obviously not meant to be played with. Some, however, are free-standing, like dolls' houses. No-one seems to know exactly what they were used for: perhaps they were merely decorative. The Museum has several.*

(Below) *A tiny wooden village made in 1922-4 by the artist David Jones for the children of his friend Eric Gill. Other artist's toys in the museum are by Roger Fry, Jessie M. King and Gerrit Rietveld.*

(Right) *A miniature kitchen in a cabinet. In an early dolls' house the kitchen is often the most interesting room because of the miniature vessels of copper, pewter, silver and ceramic which it contains. Kitchens were often made separately. This one is unusual in its arrangement and in being in a cabinet. It is thought to be Dutch, and probably dates from the seventeenth century.*

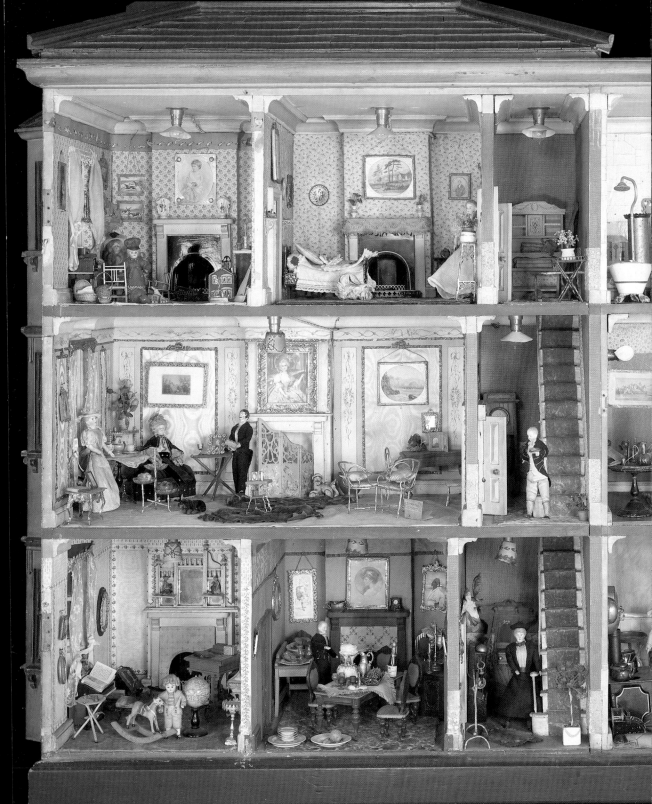

Dolls' Houses

Straight ahead from the main entrance

The earliest known dolls' house does not survive but is referred to in documents. It was made in 1558 for Duke Albrecht V of Bavaria, and was obviously not a children's toy but an expensive curiosity fit for a prince. Equally obviously, the earliest dolls' houses that do survive – some half dozen made in South Germany between 1611 and about 1700 – were made for middle-class families and were intended to assist girls in learning domestic economy. The only example of these on public view outside Germany is the Nuremberg house of 1673 at Bethnal Green.

(Left) *Miss Miles's dolls' house, made when Amy Miles was a child in the 1890s. A late Victorian interior with many interesting features.*

(Below) *A dolls' house designed by the artist Jessie M. King for an exhibition of nursery furniture in Paris in 1912.*

(Bottom) *Two holiday villas, probably made in the 1930s.*

A group of Dutch houses, made between about 1670 and 1750, and now in museums at Amsterdam, Haarlem and Utrecht, also belonged to middle-class families, but are perhaps not so much toys as status symbols.

No less impressive than these are the half-dozen best English dolls' houses of the eighteenth century: those at Uppark (c.1730) and Nostell Priory (c.1740), the Blackett House at the Museum of London (c.1740), and the Tate Baby House (c.1760), which stands at the start of the new display of dolls' houses at Bethnal Green.

About thirty-five houses are displayed, dating from 1760 to the present. Some approach the accuracy of architectural models (the Modernist 'Whiteladies', for instance). Some, of the conventional cupboard shape, have a thin front layer of architecture cheerfully adapted by a carpenter. Some, crudely cobbled together and luridly painted, have the quality of folk art. Some are interesting for their outsides; most, for their interiors. Few interiors have the taste and consistency of Mrs Bryant's Pleasure, which was made for an adult; many, of course, are the imaginative creations of children. They may give insights into domestic life of past times, especially life in ordinary houses whose interiors have not been preserved. But just because these have disappeared, it is difficult to be sure whether a dolls' house truly represents real life. Almost all our dolls' houses are English, but one German example, a Puppenstube of c.1900, stands out.

(Below left) *An eighteenth-century English dolls' house, restored by the writer Denton Welch.*

(Below right) *A dolls' house made in Liverpool in 1887, and furnished by H.M. Queen Mary in 1921.*

OPPOSITE PAGE: (top) *A room in the Nuremberg house of 1673.*

OPPOSITE PAGE: (bottom) *A room in 'Mrs Bryant's Pleasure', made in the 1860s as a careful record in miniature of the furnishings of the time.*

Dolls

In the gallery to the left of the entrance

Here the dolls are arranged in roughly chronological order, and according to the materials of which they are made, because this is the most practical way of arranging a very large collection.

Dolls, being small symbols of human beings, may well have had religious significance in some civilisations. Very rarely in modern Europe: but in Catholic countries there were images of saints, and figures for cribs. More often in modern Europe dolls have been used to record or advertise women's fashions. Mostly, however, dolls have been made to be played with.

When you first meet a doll (as with a real person) you look at its face. You often do not see its body because it is dressed. Quite a lot of our dolls have been undressed, so that you can see exactly how they were made. Perhaps the older ones look to us rather strange in this state. Nonetheless, they used to be sold unclothed, and each would have a wardrobe made for it individually, perhaps by a professional dolls' dressmaker, or perhaps by its owner's mother. Many early dolls' clothes are beautifully made with microscopic hand sewing. This skill is very rare nowadays, when dolls' clothes are often mass-produced.

(Top left) *A pedlar doll, about 1830. Such dolls were probably made by or for ladies as a parlour amusement. They were popular from the 1820s to the 1860s. This one's head is carved from a pickled apple.*

(Top centre) *A fashion doll, with a bisque head, made about 1883. It is one of a set of miniature dress models, made between 1880 and 1890 by Mrs J. A. Latter Axton, designer of styles to Marshall and Snelgrove, the London store.*

(Top right) *A portrait doll, made about 1900: Lord Roberts, V C (1832-1914), army commander-in-chief in India and the Boer War. The wax head was probably made by the Pierotti family, best known of London wax doll makers.*

(Bottom left) *'Cedric', a doll with a bisque head and jointed composition body, made by Simon & Halbig of Germany in about 1903.*

(Bottom centre) *A 'Lenci' doll made by Enrico Scavini of Turin about 1935. The head and limbs are of moulded felt.*

(Bottom right) *A 'Shirley Temple' doll, modelled on the film star, and made by the Ideal Novelty and Toy Company, U.S.A. in the 1930s.*

Traditional wooden dolls, with stick-like arms and legs, were made in vast quantities in Germany in the nineteenth century. Some of the earlier English wooden dolls, made in a similar way, are much more carefully finished. They have smoothly rounded heads but sharp features, and often smile quizzically. In the early nineteenth century some German dolls had heads of papier-mâché (or 'composition'): neat, homely young ladies with braided hair, moulded in the solid papier-mâché.

Heads made of wax, an English speciality, were more usual later in the nineteenth century. Wax could be modelled very sensitively, and the best heads of solid wax can be regarded as sculpture. Heads were more generally made of a thin coating of wax over a composition base. Such heads made in the early Victorian period often possess an instantly recognizable, charmingly cheeky expression. Later Victorian wax heads, whether representing babies (baby dolls first appeared in the 1850s) or older faces, became heavily chubby, with simpering rosebud lips. When in the 1870s dolls' heads began to be made

of porcelain, they followed the same conventional style, until in 1909 one firm had the bright idea of copying a real child's face, and the 'character doll' was born. Alongside this new realism, all sorts of stylization (e.g. the droll Kewpie, the multi-ethnic Sasha) continued to be popular.

Wax or porcelain heads were often attached to bodies of stuffed kid; to make them bend in the right places they had to be constructed in strange ways. Bodies entirely of composition with ball-joints look hardly more realistic. Various kinds of plastic have made possible greater realism, though attempts to make dolls sleep, talk or perform other natural functions usually involve complicated machinery which tends to do away with realism.

For a young child the most loved doll is often the simplest and softest, and older girls, interested in fashion, like dolls which can be dressed and undressed. But there has always been a demand (from ladies rather than children?) for very ornamental dolls, designed to be looked at in glass cases, and almost destined, therefore, for a museum.

(Below left) *'Rosa Mary', her nurse, and 'Sandy'. Three dolls of 1850-60, which belonged to a girl called Isabella Grahame.*

(Below right) *Bisque-headed dolls by famous French makers.* Left; *by Bru, 1880. Middle; 'Cigarette' by Jumeau, 1880. Right: by Steiner, about 1890. Leon Casimir Bru's factory started in 1866, Pierre François Jumeau's in 1842; in 1899 they both became founder-members of the Société Française de Fabrication de Bébés et Jouets which continued to make dolls until 1958. Steiner's firm worked from 1855 until 1908.*

(Above) *An oddity. Amusement is often aroused by three dolls made in the 1930s in extravagantly eighteenth-century style, to represent characters from Sheridan's play* School for Scandal.

(Below left) *Mechanical walking dolls.* Middle: *a doll which 'walks' on three wheels, made by Steiner of Paris between 1864 and 1873.* Left: *another example, undressed and showing the mechanism,* Right: *the 'Autoperipatetikos', made by Martin and Runyon of New York between 1865 and 1867; and another example of the clockwork mechanism, which raises and lowers each foot alternately.*

(Below right) *Dolls made of vinyl. Plastic dolls became available in the 1950s, the most successful being made of vinyl, a soft plastic.* Left: *a 'walkie-talkie' doll made in England by Pedigree in about 1953.* Right: *a Sasha doll made by Trendon of Stockport. Sasha dolls are named after their designer Sasha Morgenthaler of Zurich, who meant them to look like a child 'in the age of innocence'.*

'Princess Daisy', the most popular doll in the Museum. This English wax doll was equipped with an amazing layette, and won a medal at the Amsterdam International Exhibition, 1895. She was given to H.M. Queen Mary in 1899, and later presented to the Museum.

Children's Dress (Above left) *A boy's suit, of about 1760, made of a striped silk and cotton mixture, worn with contemporary shoes of morocco leather. The late eighteenth-century child's rocking chair is of ash wood with a rush seat.*

(Above right) *A girl's printed cotton dress, over cotton pantalettes, from the early years of the nineteenth century.*

(Below left) *A girl's velvet suit (1855-60) with glacé leather shoes. The child's birchwood chair dates from about 1850.*

(Below right) *A 'Fauntleroy' suit and hat of mauve plush, dating from 1887. This type of outfit was popularized by Frances Hodgson Burnett's book* Little Lord Fauntleroy, *whose hero dressed in this way. The tricycle horse dates from 1875-80.*

The Social History of Childhood

On the top floor

It is often said that until Victorian times, children were treated as 'miniature adults'. If you think about it, it is not easy to be sure what this might mean. But if you look at historic portraits of children, you can see why people say it. Children are often pictured wearing stiff garments of costly materials which are indeed miniature versions of adult costume. However, all children's dress is, to a greater or lesser degree, a version of adult costume. Children today are dressed as miniature adults.

In fact it is quite difficult to find out how adults treated children or children felt in the past, for family life has always been private, leaving little record for historians. Children's dress is one clue to this puzzle, and the museum has a fine collection of it, covering the last three hundred years.

But there are many other clues, some of which the museum is gathering together, while others have already been collected by historians in other places.

Babies could never have been treated as miniature adults. Until a child can walk and talk, it has to be treated in a special way. Traditionally, there have been certain pieces of equipment that were very widely used for babies. In the museum, where most of the exhibits are from Europe, cradles, feeding bottles, rattles, baby-walkers and high chairs of various periods can be compared and contrasted. Instructions to mothers on how to feed and train their children have varied widely. One custom, once quite normal but now discontinued, was to farm children out to wet nurses. Another discontinued custom was swaddling: wrapping babies up into a tight parcel with long strips of cloth. Once this began to be given

up in the course of the eighteenth century, new kinds of baby-wear were invented. These are shown in the museum, right up to the 'babygro' romper suit.

In the Middle Ages, infants, once out of swaddling clothes, were dressed to distinguish their sex, like adults. But from the sixteenth century all children, both boys and girls, wore skirts. It was a great day for a boy when, at the age of four or five, he was first allowed to put on breeches. This custom, though in decline from the late eighteenth century, did not completely die out until this century.

As adults came to think of children as special and different, they invented special dress for them. Sometimes this was intended to make them seem more charming and lovable: 'Little Lord Fauntleroy' suits, for instance. Sometimes,

(Top) *Layette pin-cushions of 1787, 1838 and 1862. Before the 1880s, babies' clothes were often fastened with ordinary dressmaking pins, so pin-cushions were both decorative and useful. However, the custom of giving them to a mother-to-be persisted long after the introduction of safety pins.*

(Left) *Nursery furniture: a mid seventeenth-century high chair of inlaid oak, and an eighteenth-century baby-walker of ash and mahogany.*

PREVIOUS PAGE (left) *Childhood in the eighteenth century: a painting showing a mother, her baby, and a child in a movable chair.*

PREVIOUS PAGE (right) *An English oak cradle, dated 1641. In it, a seventeenth century wax effigy, from Spain, of a dead child.*

Three examples of contemporary learning toys for the pre-school child. The wooden posting box and stacking toy clown are Swedish, the plastic building beakers are English. These designs were first manufactured in the 1930s, and continue to be popular children's toys today.

generations ago (just as history, for many people, goes back no further than Granny's photograph album). Recently historians have found ways of testing people's memories and impressions (which are often vague or biased) against what can be accurately measured: statistics of births, marriages and deaths. Many new (sometimes contradictory) insights have resulted.

What makes up a family differs from one historical period to another, so one cannot generalize with confidence, particularly for the pre-industrial periods. Whether parents and children, uncles and aunts, grandparents and grandchildren shared a house (or even a room) depended on the economy, employment, health and fertility. Family life was also influenced by laws (especially laws of property), by religion, and by educational systems.

It is very difficult to ascertain how parents and particularly how children felt in the past. Many historians have argued that since children so often died in infancy, right up to the nineteenth century, the grief of parents, and especially of mothers, was short-lived. It is very hard to prove that this was the case, but we can say from the material evidence we have collected that parenthood was a continual struggle. While we can often only speculate about the feelings the objects in the museum provoked in their owners, particularly children, we can document with some authority the material conditions and context that originally surrounded them.

We shall explore these and other themes in a new gallery: 'Growing Up: The Lives of Children Across the Centuries'.

as with school uniform, it marked out their position in life.

Education is a very significant part of childhood, which the museum can only touch on, chiefly through educational toys. For centuries the growing child has been helped to read and write by such toys. It is only relatively recently that the influence of child psychologists has led to the production of toys designed to train infants in bodily movement.

In the end, we can understand childhood only through understanding family life. We all have an ideal of family life, which is often our rose-tinted memory of what happened a couple of

The Museum has a large research library of historic and contemporary children's books, the Renier Collection, though little of this is on display except in special exhibitions. One such exhibition featured girls' school stories, such as Winifred Darch's book (top left), published in 1930. Among the most charming of early English children's books are miniature libraries; sets of tiny books in little bookcases. Probably the first was The Juvenile or Child's Library (top right), published by John Marshall in 1800.

(Bottom left) Along with its collection of childen's dress, the Museum possesses examples of children's needlework, such as this album of samplers, made in 1852-4.

(Bottom right) The Museum has a large collection of miniature crockery, both for children and for dolls. These cups and saucers date from the 1930s.

Ethnic Toys

*The Museum has a small
collection of 'ethnic' or folk toys
from various countries. It is
quite wide-ranging and
colourful, but does not attempt
to be a complete survey of the
world's toys. Some of the toys
are simple, like the South
African bead doll (top) or the
Mexican ten-piece band
(bottom right), made of
plaited palm leaf quite recently
but in the traditional way.
Others are examples of highly
sophisticated craftsmanship,
such as the samurai dolls for the
Japanese Boys Festival (top
right). Particularly attractive
are wooden folk toys painted in
traditional designs like the
Indian elephant bearing
passengers in a howdah, made
in Kondapalli (left). This, like
the Japanese warriors, dates
from early this century.*

(Below) *The toy as modern art: a child's buggy designed in 1918 by the Dutch designer Gerrit Rietveld (1888-1965).*

(Bottom right) *There are many craft toymakers in Britain today, most of them producing brightly painted wooden toys. The revival of interest in this traditional way of toymaking was inspired by the artist-craftsman Sam Smith (1908-83): the Museum has several examples of his work. The toys by modern craftsmen in this group are; (in front) 'Alice in Wonderland' chess set by Robin and Nell Dale, 1983; (behind) acrobats by Peter de Wit, 1983; jumping frog, boat and paddle doll by the Blue Cat Toy Co., 1982; lifeboat by Mark and Gillian Heal, 1979; 'The Royal Wedding Charger' made by Maggie Wareham to celebrate the marriage of the Prince of Wales, 1981; zoo box and animals by Jim Edmiston, 1983.*

(Top right) *One of the treasures of the Museum is an illustrated sample book, dating from about 1840, of a German toy wholesale firm, Louis and Eduard Lindner of Sonneberg. The hand-coloured lithographic illustrations give a comprehensive survey of toys available at the time, including (as shown here) soldiers, squeaking birds and miniature villages, all packed in the usual round-cornered boxes. Early German toy catalogues of this kind are rare, and almost all are in German museums.*

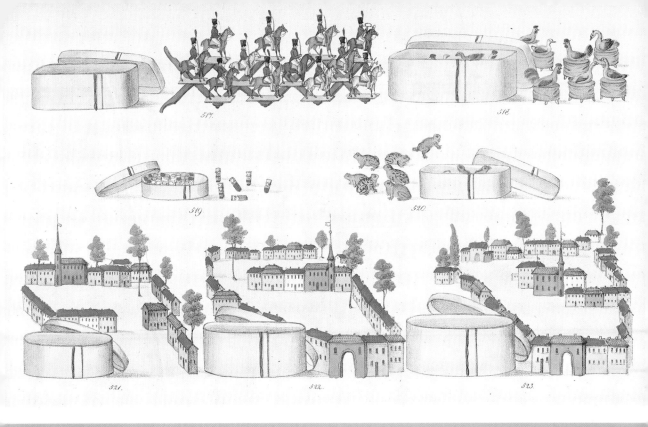

The History of the Museum

The Bethnal Green Museum was opened by H.R.H. the Prince of Wales on 24 June, 1872. The building which he opened was, however, partly second-hand. The outer shell of brick was new (and, indeed, has never been finished off, for it was intended to have at the front a colonnaded cloister garden, a clock tower, and various additional buildings) but the iron frame of the building, which gives the interior its special character, had already been used at South Kensington.

The 'Museum of Ornamental Art', which had occupied Marlborough House from 1852, moved in 1857 to a new site in Brompton and became the 'South Kensington Museum' (later to become the Victoria and Albert Museum). It needed a building in a hurry, so a prefabricated structure was run up by the firm of Charles Young & Co., which specialized in such quick buildings. It was made of iron girders and columns, with walls of corrugated iron (painted in green and white stripes) and a glass roof. It served the Museum fairly well for ten years (although scornfully called the 'Brompton Boilers') until some more solid buildings were ready. Then the Director, Henry Cole, had the idea of giving it away in pieces (for it was as easily dismantled as assembled) to local

(Right) *The Food Collection in the 'Brompton Boilers' at Kensington, before the collection and the building moved to Bethnal Green.*

(Below) *The Museum as it might have been. J. W. Wild's design for a cloister, clock tower and other buildings at the front of the main museum. These were never built.*

authorities in London who wanted to found their own museums.

Only in the East End did a group of enthusiasts take up Cole's offer. The Rector of Bethnal Green, the Rev. Septimus Hansard, together with Sir Antonio Brady and a group of subscribers including two local brewers, Messrs. Truman, Hanbury, Buxton & Co. and Messrs. Charrington, bought a piece of land (previously held in trust for the poor), converted it by special Act of Parliament to museum use, and presented it as a site for the museum. The greater part of the 'Brompton Boilers' was re-erected there in 1868, and the new shell was designed by Henry Scott, head of the South Kensington design office, with J.W. Wild (best remembered today as architect of Christ Church, Streatham). The iron construction is now of notable importance to architectural history, for although the glass-house method pioneered by Sir Joseph Paxton in the 1851 Exhibition building was widely used for railway stations and markets in the later nineteenth century, very few examples survive from as early as 1857.

Cole intended that the local people should run the museum, but they handed the task back to the South Kensington Museum. So the Bethnal Green Museum has never been a museum of local life (though in 1872 no-one suggested it should be). It has always been regarded as a way of sharing with the disadvantaged East End some of the national heritage gathered together in South Kensington. Rapid expansion had made the South Kensington Museum a very miscellaneous collection, and Bethnal Green took after it. Two popular scientific collections, which had come to South Kensington from the Great Exhibition, were moved to Bethnal Green. One was devoted to Food (explaining the chemical constituents of foodstuffs, and teaching good dietary principles), the other to Animal Products (a mix of natural history and industry, showing what useful things could be made of fur, feathers, bones etc). Art was represented, to begin with, by a loan collection: the paintings and decorative art belonging to Sir Richard Wallace. This later (1897) became a national museum in its own right, but 1872 was its first public showing in England. Consisting chiefly of priceless luxurious French eighteenth century art, it was a rich diet for the poor people of Bethnal Green.

Over the next thirty years many other private collections were loaned to the museum for exhibition for a few years. Thus it happened that Bethnal Green helped in the birth of several national museums: not only the Wallace Collection, but also the National Portrait Gallery (which was developed out of the National Portraits Exhibition, shown here in 1885) and the Tate Gallery (which grew from the Royal Academy's Chantrey Bequest, shown here in 1896).

Attendances after the first six months reached the astonishing total of 901,464; they settled down to an average of about 400,000 per year, encouraged without doubt by the fact that the museum opened in the evenings.

The huge South Kensington Museum was re-organized as a specialist art museum in 1899 and renamed the Victoria and Albert. When Bethnal Green re-opened after closure during the First World War, it fell to the new curator, A.K. Sabin, to bring the branch museum into line. The remnants of the Food Collection (much had decayed) went in Spring 1923, most of the Animal Products in 1928. The rest of the museum was re-arranged in accordance with the policy of the then Director, Sir Eric Maclagan, to devote the museum chiefly to nineteenth century art, and especially to what was relevant to the main local trades: furniture making, shoemaking, and silk weaving.

It was never easy to give a definite role to Bethnal Green so long as it was regarded as a small-scale copy of the Victoria and Albert Museum. Sir Trenchard Cox (Director 1956-66) decided that it should be a museum of English costume, while Sir John Pope-Hennessy (Director 1967-73) made it part of the Circulation Department, a London showplace for the Victoria and Albert Museum's travelling exhibitions.

It was Sabin who set the museum on the path it now follows. Taking his cue from Sir Cecil Harcourt Smith (Director 1909-24), who arranged a special children's exhibition at the Victoria and Albert Museum in 1915, Sabin tried in many ways to increase the usefulness of the museum to children. With the co-operation of the L.C.C. Education Authority, he arranged special talks for school parties, introducing a guide-lecturer in May 1924; and set up a class room in April 1925. More significantly he followed up a successful children's exhibition in 1923 by establishing a Children's Section. Here, with the help of distinguished patrons such as H.M. Queen Mary, Mrs T.T. Greg and Mrs Walter Tate, he laid the foundations of the present toy collection.

Through various changes of policy, the Children's Section continued to grow, and when Sir Roy Strong became Director of the Victoria and Albert Museum in 1974, he decided that the museum should devote itself entirely to childhood. To the toy collection would be added children's books, children's dress and any other objects associated with childhood in the Victoria and Albert Museum's collections. This means that Bethnal Green no longer tries to be a small-scale copy of the Victoria and Albert Museum. It is now a proper Victoria and Albert Museum department, responsible for its own distinct collections. While these are an integral part of the Victoria and Albert Museum, they can be kept separately at Bethnal Green without impairing the collections at South Kensington. And they give to the museum a function for which its building is particularly well suited.

The toy collection has been completely redisplayed. The organization of the children's book collection, behind the scenes, will not be completed for some time yet. The next development which visitors will notice will be on the top floor, where we shall create galleries devoted to the social history of childhood.

Mr. F. Wilson, guide lecturer, teaching a school party in 1926.

The Museum at Work

About thirty-five people work in the Museum. Visitors most easily notice the security staff, who not only look after the safety of the exhibits but also help visitors in all sorts of ways. Visitors may also meet the staff in the shop, the people who sit at a reception desk at busy times like school holidays, and, perhaps, the cleaners.

The curators are less noticeable because they spend most of their time behind the scenes. Their main task is concerned with the exhibits. They take care of all the things the Museum already has, both those on display in the galleries and those which, for various reasons, are kept in store. The curators keep records of the exhibits: what they are, where they came from, where we have put them. They find out more about them by doing research, in the Museum and in other museums and libraries. The Museum adds about 500 new objects to its collections each year. Most of these are donated, some purchased. The curators deal with all these.

It is the curators who choose and arrange the exhibits in the galleries, and write the labels about them. This can be a very big job, though some visitors seem almost to think that the exhibits arrange themselves. The temporary exhibitions are also arranged by the curators. As specialists in the various subjects the Museum deals with, the curators give information and advice to inquirers, usually by letter. They will also give opinions (but *not* valuations) on objects belonging to members of the public, provided that these are brought to the Museum and that they are the kind of thing the Museum deals with. (It is best to make an appointment in advance, since the curator you need to see may not be instantly available.)

Visitors often think that the Museum must have a workshop, where gnome-like toymakers repair broken exhibits. But it doesn't. We do have a craftsman, who helps with displaying exhibits, and a photographer. But restoration work is done for us by the Conservation Department of our parent museum, the Victoria and Albert. Building maintenance, accounts and many other things are also done for us by the V&A.

(Below left) *A curator records some new arrivals. All these soft toys were given by the same owner.*

Although museums are dedicated to preserving the past, they do change their own appearance, in order to stay attractive to people of the present. Compare the main hall of the Museum in the 1950s (above left) *with a recent view* (above right), *in the opposite direction.*

(Below centre) *Seeking guidance from a museum attendant.*

(Below right) *The front of the museum with the sign designed by artist-craftsman Howard Raybould in 1990.*

Address Cambridge Heath Road, London E2 9PA (close to Bethnal Green Underground Station)

Telephone 0181-980 2415 (recorded information) 0181-983 5200 (administration)

How to get there Underground: Bethnal Green (Central Line – one stop east from Liverpool Street).
Buses: 106, 253, D6 (Cambridge Heath Road); 8, 309 (Roman Road); 26, 48, 55 (Hackney Road).

Opening Hours Mon to Thur and Sat 10.00-17.50; Sun 14.30-17.50.

Closed every Friday, May Day Bank Holiday, Christmas Eve, Christmas Day, Boxing Day and New Year's Day.

Admission Free

Services
Café serving salads, sandwiches, cakes, children's lunch boxes, and hot and cold drinks, and offering children's birthday parties.
Shop selling souvenirs, books, T-shirts, postcards and toys.
Schools programme leaflet available from the Bookings Secretary.
Children's holiday events and Saturday workshops ring the information line for details.
Guided tours for adult groups may be booked in advance with the Bookings Secretary.

Access
The Museum has steps throughout. Help is available **but must be arranged in advance** by phone. There is a wheelchair accessible toilet (two steps down from Museum's main floor and three steps up from the entrance).

A group of early nineteenth-century figures of wood and papier-mâché, made in Germany, probably at Sonneberg.